# you're never too old to...

summersdale

YOU'RE NEVER TOO OLD TO...

First published in 2011

This revised edition copyright © Summersdale Publishers Ltd, 2017

Summersdale Publishers Ltd
46 West Street
Chichester
West Sussex
PO19 1RP
UK

www.summersdale.com

Printed and bound in Croatia

ISBN: 978-1-78685-003-4

to Rita ...............
HAPPY 60TH
'LITTLE BRO'
love
from Paul & Pauline
xx

you're never
too old to...

you're never
too old to...

... lick all the
chocolate off your
biscuit first.

you're never
too old to...

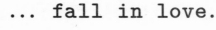

... fall in love.

The world is your
oyster. It's up
to you to find
the pearls.

Chris Gardner

you're never
too old to...

... write letters
to your heroes
about why you
admire them.

you're never
too old to...

... feed the ducks.

you're never
too old to...

... wear sequins.

you're never
too old to...

... dance all night
- or at least until
the neighbours
start to complain!

Life is being
on the wire,
everything else
is just waiting.

Karl Wallenda

you're never
too old to...


... surf the
internet.

you're never
too old to...

... begin with
dessert, move
to the main course
and finish with
a starter.

The question isn't
who is going to
let me; it's who is
going to stop me.

Ayn Rand

you're never
too old to...

... try a new sport,
like sky-diving.

you're never
too old to...

... give an
unexpected present
to a friend.

you're never
too old to...

... be called
'young man' or
'young lady'
by *somebody*.

you're never
too old to...

... learn something
silly, like
backwards writing.

You can do
anything if
you have
enthusiasm.

Henry Ford

you're never
too old to...

... try a new type
of cheese.

you're never
too old to...

... tickle a
dog's tummy.

The universe has
no restrictions.
You place
restrictions on the
universe with your
expectations.

Deepak Chopra

you're never
too old to...

... do a striptease!

you're never
too old to...

... go to see
the penguins
at the zoo.

you're never
too old to...

... act like
a teenager.

Only those who
will risk going too
far can possibly
find out how far
one can go.

T. S. Eliot

you're never
too old to...

... eat another
piece of cake.

The best is
yet to be.

Robert Browning

you're never
too old to...

... dance
the tango.

you're never
too old to...

... prefer diamonds.

you're never
too old to...

... take up yoga.

you're never
too old to...

... be a master of
the air guitar.

It always seems
impossible until
it's done.

Nelson Mandela

you're never
too old to...

... go inside the
Great Pyramid.

you're never
too old to...

... throw a party.

It is never too
late to be what you
might have been.

George Eliot

you're never
too old to...

... write a
bestseller.

you're never
too old to...

... do something
daring.

you're never
too old to...

... wear patterned
socks.

you're never
too old to...

... plant a tree
and dedicate it
to someone.

The best time to plant a tree was 20 years ago. The second best time is now.

Chinese proverb

you're never
too old to...

... ride a tandem.

you're never
too old to...


... make silly
faces at people
when they're
not looking.

Forever is composed
of nows.

Emily Dickinson

you're never
too old to...

... lie under a big
tree (blankets are
allowed) and spend
an hour just gazing
up at the branches.

you're never
too old to...

... consider roller
skates as a mode of
transport.

you're never
too old to...

... watch the waves
rolling into shore.

you're never
too old to...

... touch an
iceberg.

May you live
every day of
your life.

Jonathan Swift

you're never
too old to...

... avoid the
cracks in the
pavement.

you're never
too old to...


... give someone
flowers.

Light tomorrow
with today.

Elizabeth Barrett
Browning

you're never
too old to...

... get on the next
train out of town
and get off at
somewhere new.

you're never
too old to...

... laugh. Think
about something
that made you
laugh and giggle
all over again.

you're never
too old to...

... win the lottery.
How would you
spend it?

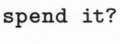

you're never
too old to...

... spend an
entire summer
day barefoot.

Be present in
all things and
thankful for
all things.

Maya Angelou

you're never
too old to...

... count your
blessings.

you're never
too old to...

... take up fencing.

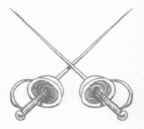

You are never too
old to set another
goal or to dream
a new dream.

Les Brown

you're never
too old to...

... go up
in a hot-air
balloon.

you're never
too old to...

... dye your hair
pink and get a
tattoo.

you're never
too old to...

... be a
fashionista.

you're never
too old to...

... travel first
class and treat
yourself to
lunch in the
dining car.

All life is an
experiment. The
more experiments
you make
the better.

Ralph Waldo Emerson

you're never
too old to...

... design a space
rocket.

you're never
too old to...

... work in a
homeless shelter
for a day.

Live the actual
moment. Only this
moment is life.

Thích Nhất Hạnh

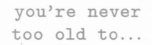

... walk down the
street bopping
your head to the
latest tunes.

you're never
too old to...

... wear high heels.

you're never
too old to...


... eat a
Knickerbocker
Glory.

The soul's joy
lies in doing.

Percy Bysshe Shelley

you're never
too old to...

... have a crush on
a film star.

you're never
too old to...

... learn to
meditate.

Live each day as
if your life had
just begun.

Johann Wolfgang
von Goethe

you're never
too old to...

... climb to the
top of a tower and
admire the view.

you're never
too old to...

... go skinny-dipping.

you're never
too old to...

... stay in
the honeymoon
suite of your
favourite hotel.

you're never
too old to...

... write a poem.

Life shrinks or
expands according
to one's courage.

Anaïs Nin

you're never
too old to...

... be whisked off
your feet.

you're never
too old to...

... become a
wine buff.

You can do
anything you set
your mind to.

Benjamin Franklin

you're never
too old to...

... sit on
Santa's knee.

you're never
too old to...

... go wild at
a rock festival.

you're never
too old to...


... learn a new
language.

you're never
too old to...

... try sushi for
the first time.

It is either easy
or impossible.

Salvador Dalí

you're never
too old to...

... wear a flower
in your hair.

you're never
too old to...

... discover that
you actually *do*
like Marmite.

you're never
too old to...


... go blonde.

you're never
too old to...

... drink a
milkshake through
a straw and make
loud bubbly sounds
when you get to the
bottom of the glass.

Every great dream
begins with
a dreamer.

Harriet Tubman

you're never
too old to...

... offer
to help
someone.

you're never
too old to...

... build a
sandcastle.

Life is a great big
canvas, and you
should throw all
the paint on
it you can.

Danny Kaye

you're never
too old to...

... get into a new
style of music.

you're never
too old to...

... run that race.

you're never
too old to...

... make someone's
day.

you're never
too old to...

... be cheeky.

The best way to
predict the future
is to create it.

Abraham Lincoln

you're never
too old to...

... watch the
sun rise.

you're never
too old to...

... do a
silly walk.

Let your joy be
in your journey –
not in some
distant goal.

Tim Cook

you're never
too old to...

... get in touch
with an old friend.

you're never
too old to...

... send a
Valentine's card.

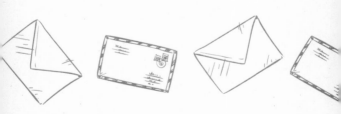

you're never
too old to...

... have a flutter
on the horses.

you're never
too old to...

... eat something
naughty but nice.

Throw caution
to the wind and
just do it.

Carrie Underwood

you're never
too old to...

... climb a tree.

you're never
too old to...

... kiss someone for
the first time.

Do one thing
every day that
scares you.

Eleanor Roosevelt

you're never
too old to...

... jump down the
last step.

you're never
too old to...

... invent a
new cocktail.

you're never
too old to...

... take a gap year.

you're never
too old to...

... have champagne
for breakfast.
Buck's Fizz is
practically orange
juice anyway.

Why did we wait
for any thing? -
Why not seize the
pleasure at once?

Jane Austen

you're never
too old to...

... dream about
being able
to fly.

Do anything,
but let it
produce joy.

Henry Miller

you're never
too old to...

... have whipped
cream and
sprinkles.

you're never
too old to...

... have a beautiful
man or woman
on each arm.

you're never
too old to...

... go back
to school.

you're never
too old to...

... stay up
late watching
horror films.

Happiness, not in another place but this place... not for another hour, but this hour.

Walt Whitman

you're never
too old to...

... get into clutter
clearing.

you're never
too old to...

... have a second
dinner.

you're never
too old to...

... tell a stranger
that they look
fantastic.

you're never
too old to...

... turn up
the music.

What is done
in love is
done well.

Vincent Van Gogh

you're never
too old to...

... fall briefly
in love with your
waiter or waitress.

you're never
too old to...

... start a conga
line.

Life isn't about
finding yourself.
Life is about
creating yourself.

George Bernard Shaw

you're never
too old to...

... slip into
something 'more
comfortable'.

Wait not till
tomorrow;
Gather the roses
of life today.

Pierre de Ronsard

you're never
too old to...

... sit at the
front of the
roller coaster.

you're never
too old to...

... perfect the
art of toasting
marshmallows on a
campfire.

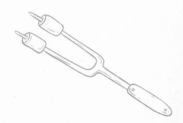

If not us, who?
If not now, when?

John F. Kennedy

you're never
too old to...

... enjoy Paris
in springtime.

you're never
too old to...

... make it
a double.

you're never
too old to...

... order it shaken,
not stirred.

you're never
too old to...

... ask someone
to dance.

you're never
too old to...

... be King
or Queen of
the BBQ.

you're never
too old to...

... be at the
front of the gig,
even if it's in a
concert hall, not a
stadium.

Life is either a
daring adventure
or nothing.

Helen Keller

you're never
too old to...

... have a stick-on
moustache for
every day of the
week. Monday is
the 'Selleck'.

you're never
too old to...

... invent the
ultimate sandwich.
The 'One of Each',
anyone?

Pearls don't lie on
the seashore. If
you want one, you
must dive for it.

Chinese proverb

you're never
too old to...

... beat your
personal best.

you're never
too old to...

... get butterflies
in your stomach.

you're never
too old to...

... be someone's
hero.

you're never
too old to...

... make your
dreams come
true.

The only reason
to be alive is
to enjoy it.

Rita Mae Brown

If you're interested in finding out more about our books, find us on Facebook at **Summersdale Publishers** and follow us on Twitter at **@Summersdale**.

## www.summersdale.com